Life Story Books for Adopted Children

of related interest

First Steps in Parenting the Child who Hurts
Tiddlers and Toddlers
Caroline Archer
ISBN 978 1 85302 801 4

Next Steps in Parenting the Child Who Hurts
Tykes and Teens
Caroline Archer
ISBN 978 1 85302 802 1

Nurturing Attachments
Supporting Children who are Fostered or Adopted
Kim S. Golding
ISBN 978 1 84310 614 2

Big Steps for Little People
Parenting Your Adopted Child
Celia Foster
Forewords by David Howe and Daniel A. Hughes
ISBN 978 1 84310 620 3

Great Answers to Difficult Questions about Adoption
What Children Need to Know
Fanny Cohen Herlem
ISBN 978 1 84310 671 5

The Child's Own Story
Life Story Work with Traumatized Children
Richard Rose and Terry Philpot
Foreword by Mary Walsh, co-founder and Chief Executive of SACCS
ISBN 978 1 84310 287 8

Connecting with Kids through Stories
Using Narratives to Facilitate Attachment in Adopted Children
Denise B. Lacher, Todd Nichols and Joanne C. May
ISBN 978 1 84310 797 2

New Families, Old Scripts
A Guide to the Language of Trauma and Attachment in Adoptive Families
Caroline Archer and Christine Gordon
ISBN 978 1 84310 258 8

Life Story Books for Adopted Children

A Family Friendly Approach

Joy Rees

Foreword by Alan Burnell
Illustrated by Jamie Goldberg

Jessica Kingsley Publishers
London and Philadelphia

First published in 2009
by Jessica Kingsley Publishers
116 Pentonville Road
London N1 9JB, UK
and
400 Market Street, Suite 400
Philadelphia, PA 19106, USA

www.jkp.com

Copyright © Joy Rees 2009
Foreword copyright © Alan Burnell 2009
Illustrations copyright © Jamie Goldberg 2009

Library of Congress Cataloging in Publication Data

Rees, Joy.
  Life story books for adopted children : a family friendly approach / Joy Rees ; foreword by Alan Burnell ; illustrated by Jamie Goldberg.
     p. cm.
  Includes bibliographical references (p.   ) and index.
  ISBN 978-1-84310-953-2 (pb : alk. paper) 1. Adopted children--Family relationships. 2. Diaries (Blank-books) I. Title.
  HV875.R36 2009
  362.734--dc22

                                                    2008040884

British Library Cataloguing in Publication Data
A CIP catalogue record for this book is available from the British Library

ISBN 978 1 84310 953 2

Printed and bound in Great Britain by
Athenaeum Press, Gateshead, Tyne and Wear

To my mother - always such a loving, playful and skilful storyteller!

Acknowledgements

Many thanks to my husband Gwyn, my sister Janet and my favourite niece, Jo. Their enthusiasm, support and advice have been invaluable.

Much gratitude also goes to my ex-colleagues in the Adoption Support Team at Surrey for their encouragement, and to Alan Burnell at Family Futures, who read the first draft, saw the potential and suggested publication.

A big thank you to Jamie for his illustrations.

Last, but certainly not least, I am indebted to the many adopted adults, adoptive parents and wonderful children I have enjoyed meeting over the years. They have been truly inspirational!

Contents

Foreword

This brave little book addresses one of the more complex issues in social work today. Preparing life story books for children became part of social work practice in the 1970s. At that time they were designed to give young adopted children a sense of continuity and identity. There was research evidence at the time that suggested that, because of the closed nature of adoption, young people and adults who had been adopted as babies suffered from 'genealogical bewilderment'.

However, the population of children who are placed for adoption today invariably have experienced adverse and traumatic environments in infancy. We now realize that such children suffer developmental trauma as a consequence. Joy Rees' book is designed to help social workers construct life story books that acknowledge those early difficult experiences in an honest and open way. Joy's advice on how to do this is based on her understanding of how early trauma affects children's memory and their ability to regulate themselves, hence her recommendation that parents should be involved in the process. We have learned from attachment theory that children who are adopted need to develop 'a coherent narrative' and Joy's book endeavours to provide a format in which social workers can help children and parents do this together.

I recommend this book to social workers who have the complex task of compiling life story books for adopted children. The simplicity of its approach belies the sophistication of the thinking and theory that lies behind it.

Alan Burnell
Co-Director of Family Futures
2008

Introduction

Compiling life story books for adopted children has been part of good social work practice for the last 30 years, though early life books were little more than scrap books or photograph albums. Recent versions tend to give a more coherent narrative, and, using a selection of photographs, drawings, diagrams and documents, provide a very detailed account of a child's life journey.

In essence, life story books should provide answers to the many questions children are likely to have – but may be reluctant to ask – about their early life experiences, prior to their adoptions. The what happened, when and why questions.

As Vera Fahlberg (2003) says, a life story book is basically 'a chronology of the child's life, helping the young person to understand and remember what has happened to him or her in the past' (p.354).

Having a clear understanding of his or her own history is seen as 'grounding' and of paramount importance as this enables the child to live more comfortably in the present and to plan for the future.

It is now generally agreed that the main aims of a life story book are:

- to give details and understanding of the child's history

- to build the child's sense of identity

- to enable the child to share their past with their adopters and others

- to give a realistic account of early events and to dispel fantasies about the birth family

- to link the past to the present and to help both the child and the adopter to understand how earlier life events continue to impact on behaviour

- to acknowledge issues of separation and loss

- to enable adoptive parents to understand and develop empathy for the child

- to enhance the child's self-esteem and self-worth

- to help the child to develop a sense of security and permanency

- to promote attunement and attachment.

Traditionally, to achieve these aims, life story books have started with the child's past – often unintentionally but inevitably feeding directly into the trauma and into the child's sense of shame and blame. This could be avoided by starting with the present and the adoptive parents. My approach allows the child to explore past trauma from the safety of a secure base.

Chapter 1

A New Approach

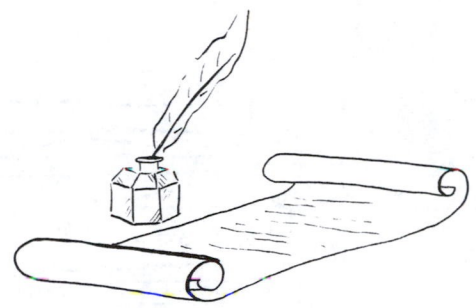

The traditional approach: Past → Present

A life story book is an essential 'tool' that an adoptive parent can use to help their child gain a sense of identity and an understanding of their history. To achieve this, the book usually starts with the child's birth and details of the birth family, and progresses chronologically to the present, ending with the adoption. As Beth O'Malley (2004) stresses, 'A lifebook starts with the child's birth, not their arrival into their adoptive family' (p.8).

This traditional structure often proves uncomfortable for both adoptive parent and child. It may be too direct, threatening or painful and, as a consequence, the book is often put away or damaged. This suggests that a different approach to the construction of life story books is needed.

By changing the format the book can be used primarily to encourage secure family attachments and a sense of permanency, and ultimately this may be far more effective in helping children to acquire a more positive and integrated sense of identity and a greater understanding of their history.

A new approach: Present → Past → Present → Future

'Our sense of self is closely dependent on the few intimate attachment relationships we have or have had in our lives, especially our relationship with the person who raised us' (Bowlby 2007, p.viii). Furthermore, a child's sense of history and identity needs time to 'evolve'. This will happen in a less threatening and more positive way if life story books concentrate on facilitating healthy attachments and on giving the children a sense of permanency and security.

To achieve this, the book should start not with the child's past but with the present; and end not with the present and the adoption, but with a hopeful and encouraging future.

Designing the book so that the child's history is in the middle is symbolically significant. The history is not only shared openly, it is literally contained and embraced by their adoptive family, so it may feel safer and more manageable for the child.

The past should not overwhelm the child and the history should be kept honest but short – in perspective in terms of the child's whole life. They have a long future ahead!

Chapter 2

A Life Story Book is Not...

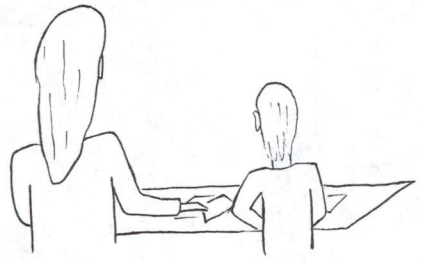

Life Story Work

There is sometimes confusion between life story work and a life story book. Life story work is generally considered to be the process of helping a child understand his or her history, while the book is regarded as the end product. Using a variety of approaches – listening, talking, drawing, painting, playing, storytelling, compiling ecomaps, family trees or other diagrams, or using sand trays, puppets and interactive packages – life story work aims to help children to remember their life journey and unravel their confusions and misunderstandings about their past. 'Life story work is an attempt to give back some of this past to children separated from their families of origin' (Ryan and Walker 2007, p.3). It is about processing and internalizing the information. It is also seen as 'a therapeutic tool that deals with the child's inner world and how that relates to the child's perception of external reality' (Rose and Philpot 2005, p.15).

Fundamentally, life story work always involves the child, while the child is not always directly involved in writing the book. Indeed, Rose and Philpot (2005) acknowledge that although there are many ways of involving the child, the responsibility for writing the book is on the worker, and they also see the book as the end product and 'first and foremost, a clear account of what happened during the process of internalisation' (p.119). Certainly many elements of the life work can then be incorporated into the book. However, including too much of the actual work could confuse and distract from the child's understanding of their own story.

Many children placed with adoptive parents are too young or just too anxious to engage in life story work, and they may need the book first to allay some of their fears. The book gives the child the basic narrative, and it can then be used by professionals or by adoptive parents as the basis for future life story work. Sometimes the product needs to come first and the process of internalization follows.

Some other things a life story book is not:

- **A background history or a summary of the child's permanence report**: These reports are prepared for the Adoption Panel and other professional meetings. They give a very detailed account of the child's history. The adoptive parents should have copies of these and will be able to share the content with the child, when they feel it would be helpful. After the age of 18 years, the child can also apply to the adoption agency for access to this information.

- **A later life letter**: This is a letter addressed to the child and written by the child's social worker at the time of placement. It is given to the adoptive parents for safe keeping. The letter contains more information and factual details to be shared with the child at a later stage – during the teenage years or earlier if appropriate.

- **A chronology**: This is a list of significant people, events, changes and movements since birth/pre-birth, with dates and ages. A chronology may also be produced in the form of a life graph or flow chart.

- **A photograph album**: Whilst every effort should be made to gather photographs of birth parents, siblings, other birth relatives, foster carers and significant people in the child's life, with names, relationships and dates, they do not all need to be in the life story book. They should be kept in a separate album with a few scanned into the book.

- **A foster carers' memory book or box**: A memory book is usually a folder or ring binder with information, anecdotes, developmental milestones, photographs, cards, certificates and other mementos gathered while the child lived with the foster family. It is an extremely helpful way of preserving those precious early memories. Many foster carers are now also gathering other memorabilia – a favourite toy, item of clothing or other possessions, a lock of hair, those first milk teeth, copies of school reports, certificates, prizes and any other special trinkets or little souvenirs the child has gathered – and storing them in a customized box.

  Foster carers' memory books and boxes contain extremely important 'treasures'. For children who have experienced many moves, their histories will have become fragmented and their memories are so easily lost, so foster carers play a vital role in safeguarding these memories for the children in their care.

All of the above are important and should be given to the adoptive parents, with explanations. They can all be shared with the child when appropriate. However, none of them are substitutes for the life story book.

Chapter 3

A Different Perspective

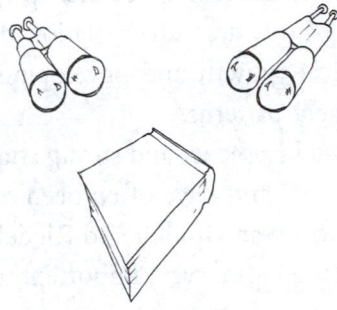

With greater understanding of attachments and of the impact of early relationships and early experiences on child development, including neurological development, it is clear that not only the format but also the focus of the life story book needs to change.

A life story book should be written in a way that reinforces a sense of permanency and stability, raises self-esteem, and promotes attunement and a secure attachment. Attachment is considered to be the bond that grows between a child and parent, while attunement is a parent's ability to understand their child's cries, sounds and facial expressions and to respond appropriately – it is the ability to see into their child's mind. Attunement is the base on which healthy, secure attachments are formed.

John Bowlby is considered to be the father of attachment theory. He maintained that human infants experience the world and their sense of self through their relationship with primary carers. All of us, from the cradle to the grave, are happiest when life is organized as 'a series of ever-lengthening excursions' from the secure base provided by those carers (Bowlby 2007, p.129). If the parent is stable and reliable, a source of safety, security and comfort, then a positive attachment will form and the child will develop a positive sense of self – and their world will be experienced as a safe place and one to be explored and enjoyed. The provision of this secure base is 'a central feature of [Bowlby's] concept of parenting' (Bowlby 1992, p.11).

Newborn babies are unable to survive alone. Their bodies and their brains are underdeveloped and they are completely dependent on a responsible adult to meet their physical and emotional needs. It is the quality of this first adult relationship that directly affects a child's psychological growth and development, and leads to secure or insecure attachment patterns.

To build a secure and strong attachment, certain types of interactions are essential and have often been referred to as the 'dance' or 'steps' of attachment (van Gulden and Riedel 1998–1999, pp.3–1).

There are three very important stages of forming a secure attachment:

- **The interactive cycle of relaxation and arousal**: If a parent consistently recognizes and responds appropriately to the baby's state and satisfies their needs, a strong foundation of trust and security is laid down.

- **The falling in love stage**: The positive interactions between the child and parents, gazing into each other's eyes, cooing, smiling and generally respecting, valuing and enjoying each other's company.

- **The belonging and claiming process**: van Gulden stresses that 'All humans need to feel that they belong in their families and that their family unit claims them' (van Gulden and Riedel 1998–1999, pp.3–9).

To be an effective tool for adoptive parents, the steps of this dance need to be reflected in the life story book and adoptive parents clearly need a much higher profile. They must be allowed to claim their children and we must enable children to feel that they belong.

Chapter 4

The Inner Child and Subliminal Messages

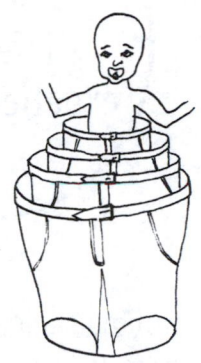

To understand the 'inner child' or the 'internal working model', we need to fully appreciate the significance of early relationships and experiences and recognize the impact that these have on a child's growth and development, and we also need to look in more detail at the different types of attachment. With this knowledge, we can raise a child's self-esteem and increase their self-worth, by ensuring that appropriate, positive subliminal messages are incorporated throughout the book.

All adopted children have experienced a primal separation and loss. Those who have also suffered neglect and abuse in their formative years are further traumatized and are often more confused about their past. Such children tend to hold themselves responsible for any ill treatment they have suffered, have low self-esteem and a deep sense of shame. Many find it difficult to trust adults or to form secure attachments.

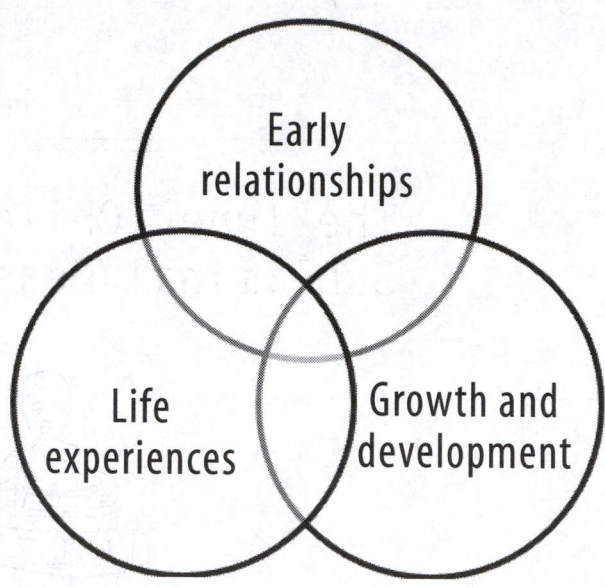

Bowlby (1992) identified the correlation between these three 'spheres' and how this affects the way children feel about themselves and how they see the world. The three spheres combine to shape a child's inner world. It is this 'inner working model', the child's core, which provides the key to understanding the child's current behaviour. In effect, a child's behaviour will tell you much about their history, and their history will explain their behaviour.

Early relationships

The quality of the first relationship is of prime importance. As this relationship begins to develop pre-birth, the first attachment is with the mother. The level and type of any parental–child attachment depends on the parent's emotional and physical availability, and on their ability to respond appropriately to the child's needs. If parents are attuned, they read their baby's signals and are able to meet his or her needs. Over time, a secure attachment is formed. Conversely, if a baby's needs are not met, an insecure attachment will form. This could be an 'avoidant', 'ambivalent' or 'disorganized' attachment.

- **Avoidant**: When a parent is consistently unresponsive and un-available to a child, and repeatedly ignores or rejects, the child eventually switches off. He or she becomes emotionally closed down, disassociates, feels unloved and avoids intimate relation-ships. There is no attunement or connection.

  These children adapt to this form of parenting by developing an emotional distance. They do not trust adults, so they become self-reliant and are often described as 'putting up a brick wall'. They need to maintain their independence, are reluctant to seek assistance and are seen as the controlling, bossy children. They may have difficulty making friends because of their intimacy issues and they fall out with those they have because of the need to be in charge.

- **Ambivalent**: If the quality of the parenting is inconsistent – one moment loving and affectionate and the next angry or agitated – the child becomes anxious and bewildered. The resulting 'mental models' are ones of unpredictability and insecurity. Having re-ceived such mixed messages from the parent, the world is now a very confusing place and life becomes an emotional roller coaster as these children experience the 'biological paradox': the adult that they need to go to for comfort and care is also the source of their anxiety.

  Despite such inconsistent parenting, these children often appear to be very attached to the parent. They are very dependent and 'clingy' as they try to remain physically close. They are reluc-tant to let the parent out of their sight in case they disappear. Such behaviour is often seen as a measure of 'good' attachment. In fact these children are constantly checking and are unsure when they will get their next meal, drink, cuddle, etc. They don't want to miss their chance, so they stay close. They are scared and anxious and as they get older they become the children who try to parent their parents. These children often remain within the family longer than is good for them as the damaging nature of their attachment is not always recognized. They are, in fact, in an emotionally lonely and fearful place and certainly deserve better parenting.

- **Disorganized**: This is the most worrying group. Children with avoidant or ambivalent attachment styles have developed some coping strategies. This third group of children is so confused that they have no effective strategies! Not only are their basic needs unmet, but they also experience their parents as very unpredictable, frightening figures. The parents' behaviour is often overwhelming and at times absolutely terrifying. These children experience an extreme version of the 'biological paradox'. This poses a great dilemma for them and they see no solution. Unable to make sense of this situation they mirror their parents' behaviour and they, too, become chaotic and disorganized. Life is exhausting as they must remain hypervigilant at all times.

Children in the three groups have some common characteristics. They have negative inner working models and blame themselves for the poor parenting they have received. Most tend to feel unlovable, have low self-esteem and an innate sense of 'badness' and shame. They feel that their early negative experiences are their fault and they do not deserve better.

Life experiences

As discussed, a baby who experiences poor, neglectful parenting will develop an insecure attachment. Inconsistent or abusive parents cause further trauma. Children of such parents learn that they cannot trust adults to care for them, and their experiences make them more vulnerable and more susceptible to stress.

Attuned, attentive parents are able to soothe their children when they are distressed and help them to regulate their emotions. A child who is not helped to develop this ability will be driven by their emotions and will have poor impulse control. For these children, the world is a confusing and frightening place and they continually live on the verge of a fight, flight or freeze response. They become sensitized to stress, and are regarded as unpredictable as they appear to overreact to particular incidents or to unknown triggers.

In such a state, a child's general development is impaired, cognitive processes are impeded and thinking logically is just not possible. This further compounds their reputation of being 'unpredictable' children.

Growth and development

So a child's ability to grow and progress through the usual stages of development will be seriously impeded if they have neglectful or abusive parenting. A secure attachment will not be established and further abuse will increase the trauma. This leads to additional stress. Without a responsive, soothing parent, emotions cannot be regulated, so the stress escalates.

Stress and anxiety use up enormous amounts of energy. This energy has to be diverted from other areas, leading to a reduced capacity for physical growth, neurological development and learning. This is evident in the child's behaviour as they struggle with common cognitive concepts that normally develop in the first few months or years of life, such as object constancy – infants gradually learn that objects, including people, have not disappeared if they cannot be touched or they are out of sight or earshot.

Such children may also have difficulty with cause and effect thinking, or be unable to grasp the concept of consequences or to see the world from other people's perspectives. This lack of flexibility of thought means that they find it hard to empathize. They therefore struggle with relationships, so have difficulty making or maintaining friends.

The inner working model

All adopted children have experienced a primal separation and loss, and they will have some attachment issues. Those who have been neglected or abused will have further difficulties resulting from their insecure attachments, and will have a very negative 'inner working model'.

Children with a negative 'inner working model' will have a low sense of self-worth, a mistrust of adults and a perception of the world as an unsafe place. They are likely to lack inner confidence and may feel worthless and unloveable. Many of these children develop an inner sense of 'shame' or 'badness', blame themselves for their early experiences, and are 'primed' to expect further abuse or neglect. These misconceptions have been 'hard wired' into their brain – laid down in their unconscious memory – and attempting to access or change these inner beliefs at a conscious level will have little effect. Just telling children they are loveable and valued will not work. They need to feel this from the inside.

The importance of subliminal messages

Because the negative inner beliefs are laid down in the child's unconscious memory, they need to be addressed on an unconscious level. With this in mind, when writing a life story book, the child's history needs to be presented in a sensitive and honest way that will help the child to understand the past while raising self-esteem, rather than making the child feel in some way responsible for the abuse or neglect, and lowering their feelings of self-worth.

Taking care to ensure that positive messages are there from the start, and threading them throughout the life story book, will begin to redress the unconscious negative feelings, and will help the child to challenge and reframe their limiting inner beliefs.

The subliminal messages throughout the child's book need to be:

- past events are not the child's fault

- he or she is loved and loveable

- he or she deserves better parenting

- he or she is claimed and belongs

- adults can be trusted and they understand.

The final message should be one of a positive and hopeful future.

Chapter 5

Involving Adoptive Parents

If the adoptive parents are to re-parent their child successfully, with empathy and with an understanding of their child's 'inner world' and the impact this has on his or her current behaviour, then they will clearly need access to a very detailed history, a chronology, and a later life letter. Although written for the child, a carefully prepared life story book will also help the adopters to see the child's story from a different perspective: the child's. 'Sharing this information and discussing it with the parents can also be a therapeutic experience for them, such that it gives them insight into their child and a greater sense of empathy' (Burnell and Vaughan 2008, p.228).

To use the book appropriately, adoptive parents need to appreciate its purpose and to understand the significance of those important subliminal messages. If they have had the opportunity to contribute and to suggest amendments to the final version, they will feel more comfortable with the content and therefore more confident about using the book. In essence, the book needs to be both child and adoptive parent friendly!

It is imperative that the adoptive parents feel able to share the important 'middle' section – the history – with their child. If they seem reluctant to read about the past with the child, this may give the impression that there is something so awful and bad in the past that the child will not be able to cope with it. In fact, whatever the past, the child has already lived through it and survived. What is sharable is bearable.

On some level, whether conscious or unconscious, the child is likely to have memories of their early neglect or abuse. Not acknowledging this could feed the child's sense of shame and increase their fear of further rejection if their 'awful secret' is discovered.

Adopters can feel confident that recalling a painful past in a safe, trusted and nurturing environment will not re-traumatize the child. On the contrary, it reassures the child that the adoptive parents already know all about them – including their past – and that they still find them loveable.

The content of the book is obviously important, but the actual process of telling the story can also help with the attunement and attachment processes. The adoptive parent's tone of voice, facial expressions and body language will all have an impact on the child. Simple clip-art illustrations of different facial expressions can be included to allow the adoptive parent and child to gently and playfully explore the links with different feelings and emotions. This is of particular significance as many adopted children have great difficulty 'reading' faces.

For young children, the adopters may read only a few of the words and the child will be more interested in the illustrations and scanned photographs. Later the words, and the feelings behind them, will become more significant.

The book may provoke a mixture of emotions for both child and adoptive parent – providing an opportunity that could be used to good effect by an attuned and empathetic adoptive parent.

Chapter 6

Compiling a Life Story Book

Remember that life letters and other reports and documents should be available to the child at a later stage. The life story book is just the first tool used to help the child to understand his or her self and history.

There are a number of points to consider when writing a life story book:

- Historical details are available from the child's file, and current information should be gathered from the adoptive parents and child. Before you begin, check names and terms used by the child and family and let them choose their own title for the life story book – 'All About Danny', 'Danny Rules OK', 'Cool Dude Danny' and 'Danny's Life Adventure' are just some of the suggestions received from children. Put the year on the title page too.

- The book is not an abridged version of the child's placement report. It must be child focused and child friendly and contain bite sized sections, with scanned photographs and plenty of colour, drawings and clip-art to illustrate events and feelings. Social work jargon, such as 'placed on the Child Protection Register under the category of emotional neglect', is meaningless to a five year old or indeed to the average adult!

- The book needs to be child sized – in other words, not so large and heavy that it is difficult for a young child to lift or hold. It also needs to be durable and child proof. Laminating the pages may seem appropriate for toddlers, but this tends to make the book very heavy. A spare copy or a CD version may be the solution.

- Use the child's first name and write in the third person, unless working with older children who are writing the story with you. For younger children, the less direct approach is a more effective and less threatening way of exploring their history. Toddlers use their names rather than 'I' or 'me' and only gradually develop a sense of self. Many adopted children function at a very young emotional age, and adopters are encouraged to 'think toddler'. Using the third person in the book mirrors this developmental process.

- Currently, the average age of children being adopted in the UK is four years old. Irrespective of age, when preparing the book, you should make it appropriate for a school-age child (roughly five to ten years old). They may already have gone through the book many times, but it is only when they start school that children begin to understand the emotional significance of their adoption. Prior to this some will assume that, just like them, everyone has been fostered and adopted.

- A school project about families and requests for baby photographs raises many issues for an adopted child. Changes in the way thoughts are processed are also occurring at this age, which can lead to further questions.

    Parents who have adopted children as babies or toddlers often notice a change in their children at this stage. Some sense an undercurrent of sadness or grumpiness, while others comment on increased concerns, difficulties, lethargy, anger or aggression. 'Attachment issues' become more apparent, and adopters may feel confused and ineffective as parents, as they begin to absorb the child's emotions.

It is at this stage that an adoptive parent will be able to use a sensitively written life story book to most effect. While reminding the adopters about the child's history, it can also be used to reassure the child and to help unravel the confused thoughts and emotions they are struggling to understand.

The format: Present → Past → Present → Future

- Beginning the story with the child's birth and with the birth parents' details and history will be overwhelming and is not a good way to promote a secure attachment between the adopters and child. In doing so, the adopters are beginning by reminding the child that they are not 'Mummy' or 'Daddy'. Think of the subliminal messages here, for both child and adopter.

  Helping the child to feel safe, contained and 'grounded' in the present is a more appropriate starting point. From this position the adoptive parent can help their child to look back and begin to make some sense of their history.

- To understand ourselves fully and move on to the future we need to understand our past, but young children live very much in the present and have a limited understanding of 'yesterday' or 'tomorrow'. Many older adopted children have a similarly fragile grasp of time, so first we need to give them a much stronger sense of their present.

1. Present

- Start the book with the present: the child as he or she is now, with scanned photographs of the adoptive family and the home.

Include a general description, a photograph of the child, and one with Mum and Dad (i.e. adoptive mum and dad). They should feature at the beginning and not be tacked on, almost as an afterthought, at the end. Do not refer to them as 'new' Mummy and Daddy – just as Mummy and Daddy, and do so throughout the book.

- Make sure there are many positive comments about the child right from the start. For example, sparkly/twinkling eyes, lovely/sunny smile or soft/shiny hair. The adopters need to be very involved, so include positive comments from them about their son or daughter and his or her talents, interests, nicknames, etc. – and interweave these positives throughout the body of the book.

  Be mindful of the subliminal messages. Children need to feel positive about themselves – that they are important, loveable and loved.

- If the child is at nursery or school, add a few comments and pictures and mention names of teachers, pick out any positive comments they have made, and mention favourite subjects and names of friends.

  If children are struggling with school there will still be positive comments to include. They may be great at helping the teacher to put things away, or good at cutting and sticking, kind to other children or amazing at cartwheels! Feed the positives and don't dwell on the negatives. The life book is not the place for this!

- For children who find separations difficult, parents may find that they are frequently asked to collect the children early from school, either because they are upset, feeling ill, or they have been disruptive in some way. Children express separation anxiety in many different ways and this issue could be alluded to indirectly by mentioning that while the child is at school his mum/dad still think about him as they are cleaning the house, shopping, working at the office, etc. Out of sight is not out of mind – and this needs to be constantly reinforced in all kinds of ways.

- Now write about the child's name and scan in a copy of the birth certificate (i.e. the new certificate showing the adoptive names). Mention the meaning or significance. This could lead to a simple explanation about the change to the child's birth name, and the concept of adoption can be introduced. For example, children join families in different ways, some are born into them, some are fostered and some are adopted etc.

- If giving examples of other people who have been fostered or adopted, make these meaningful to the child. For older children, Moses, Aristotle, Nelson Mandela, Kate Adie or Fatima Whitbread may be appropriate, but these will mean little to younger children. For a four or five year old, Superman, Stuart Little the mouse or Babe the pig will have far more of an impact. Bring in positive examples of relatives or friends within the adoptive parents' network who were also adopted. Think about the child's world and reinforce their own points of reference.

  For inter country adoptions, many children are 'abandoned' and their births not registered by birth parents. However the same format is still helpful and an honest but sensitive explanation is still needed. For example:

> Kas's mum and dad gave him the name Kasem, but it is usually shortened and he likes being called Kas. His mum and dad chose this name because it is Thai for being 'well and happy', and because they thought that it was just the right name for Kas. His middle name is Virote, and this is Thai for 'great power'. Virote is the name that was chosen for him in Thailand, before he came to live with his mum and dad in Newtown.

2. Past

- Having explored and endorsed the present for the child, it is now time to introduce the past. Start with the beginning: the child's birth.

- If there is little information about the birth, use some poetic licence – generally we can assume that babies were born gorgeous, lovely, adorable, loveable little bundles. Details of birth weight and length and time and day of birth are usually available for all domestic adoptions and should be included. If the child was premature, or unwell and in a special care unit, include details of this.

- All babies have a birth mother and a birth father, so simply say this. Give the birth mother's name and, if available, the birth father's name, and from then on refer to them using their first names only. Scan in one or two photographs if they are available. (The originals and other birth family photographs can be safely put in a separate photograph album.) There are a few cases where photographs of the birth parents should not be included in the book. For example, for children who have experienced extreme violence or sexual abuse, photographs may re-traumatize and not be appropriate.

- If the birth father's identity is not known or there is no information available, this must be acknowledged. Not mentioning a birth father could lead the child to believe the father is just so 'bad' he has to remain a secret, or the child may grow up assuming that their adoptive father is actually their birth father. For example:

> All children have a birth mother and a birth father. John's birth mother is called Susan and this is usually shortened to Sue. John's birth father is called Nigel. Very little is known about Nigel. Sue said that he was about the same age as her but much taller, around 6 ft. He had a medium build and brown hair. Nigel and Sue hadn't known each other for very long. Sue told

him that she was going to have a baby, but their friendship ended a few months before John was born and he had moved away. Sue said that he was a lorry driver and he was from Wales. He may have gone back to that area to live, but she wasn't sure.

- Most adopted children were welcomed into the world by their birth parents. The birth parent would have felt love for the child and may have breastfed, registered the birth, and chosen a name with great care and for a particular reason. All this should be mentioned.

- Give basic details of significant members of the birth family: ages, physical descriptions, ethnic and cultural information, religion, personalities, occupations, interests, hobbies and talents. Do not overload with intimate details of the birth parents' history. Keep this section positive and short.

- There has been much debate about the difference between being 'loved' and being 'loveable' and some may feel that being told that a neglectful or abusive parent loved him or her will be very confusing for a child. However, many adopted children were wanted and loved by their birth parents and it would be wrong to deny this, even if those same parents were later unable to parent the child appropriately. We need to be more creative about the way we explain and explore the nature of love and parenting within life story books.

- There needs to be a sensitive and honest account of the events and concerns leading to the child's relinquishment or removal from the birth parents. Neglect or abuse needs to be explained in a very simple and non-judgemental way. Comments about the birth mother's 'inability to meet your physical and emotional needs' will mean nothing to a child.

  For example, children understand their basic needs, such as the need for food and clothing, or to go to school, or for lots of cuddles as a baby. They need to know that their birth parent simply didn't know how to look after them properly, and certainly not in the way that such a precious and loveable child deserved.

- For inter country adoptions there is often little or no information about birth family and a sensitive and honest approach is needed in this section. For example:

> Kas was born in Thailand, and like all babies he had a birth mother and birth father, although very little is known about them. They were both from Thailand and just like Kas they would have had lovely dark shiny hair and brown eyes and skin.
>
> Kas's birth mother may have been very young or very poor, as a few days after Kas was born she decided that she wouldn't be able to look after him properly, so she took him to a baby's nursery in Cha-Am.
>
> She must have carried Kas there and carefully placed him in a little basket, near the entrance to the nursery, so the nurses who looked after the babies would be sure to see him. She would have known that they would take good care of him. And this is exactly what happened. When the nursery nurse saw him she picked him up very gently. She looked all around but they were not able to find Kas's birth mother anywhere. The police came too and they searched, but they could not find anyone either.
>
> Kas was a beautiful and very loveable baby. He was very healthy and the social workers who came to see him at the nursery and the nannies who looked after him all agreed that he was indeed a really gorgeous little bundle. They chose the Thai name Virote for him as it means 'powerful' and they all agreed that he was indeed a very strong little baby, so the name seemed just right for him.

- Giving an honest account of the circumstances leading to their adoption, while acknowledging sadness and loss, should make it clear that any neglect or abuse was not the child's fault. Words need to be carefully chosen to ensure that they do not feed into the child's sense of blame and shame.

- Lengthy accounts of the birth parent's unhappy childhood, and explanations of the 'root cause' of their difficulties, should not be in the child's book. Children may feel somehow responsible for the birth parent's sadness or inadequacies, and believe that as the abuse or neglect was not really their birth parent's fault, it must be theirs – again reinforcing their sense of 'badness'.

- Information about case conferences, care proceedings and specific dates is not needed. Keep these details for the later life letter and other reports that will be available to the child when older. They will over-complicate and actually detract from the child's understanding of their story.

- Give information and photographs about the foster carers – but again not too much, as children should now be given a memory book or box of their time with the carers. If there were several fostering placements, this is usually due to the carers' other commitments, so choose words carefully to ensure that the child does not think that they were moved to other foster carers or to the adoptive parents for 'being naughty'.

- Bring the story back to the adopters. Again, protracted explanations about 'Adoption Panels' and 'Matching Meetings' are not needed. There is usually a photograph of the child's first meeting with the adopters and they themselves may have positive comments about this to quote in the book. Some adopters say 'It was love at first sight' or they have another positive memory or anecdote to tell. Usually at this stage, the children in photographs look tense and anxious, so avoid captions about how happy and delighted the child was to have a 'new mummy and daddy'. While it might be appropriate to comment on the adopters' sense of joy, acknowledge the understandable ambivalence of the child.

- Give some details of the move to the adopters' home, including how strange it must have been for the child at first. Comment on all the different things the child had to get used to – different people, a different house, a different bedroom, different food, different words for things, different smells and sounds, different feelings, different colours and furniture, different nursery/school and so on. So many differences!

- Comment on the adoptive parents' knowledge and understanding of the child, and how they knew about all the things needed to keep a child happy, healthy and safe. It may be appropriate to mention that they also realized that some of the child's previous experiences may have left him or her feeling worried, wobbly, upset, cross, angry or sad. This could provide an opportunity for the adoptive parent to explore facial expressions and feelings with the child.

- Writing the book in the third person also affords more opportunity for gentle or playful conjecture with regard to the child's emotions. 'I expect that John may have felt...' or 'I wonder if John felt...' allows for further discussion between the child and parent. The child can either identify with or reject the suggested feelings.

- If the child has particular problems, such as bed-wetting, nightmares or eating difficulties, this could be tentatively explored via the book – but never in direct reference to the child. For example:

> If children keep all their worries inside, their inside soon becomes so full it just can't hold them all in! These scary feelings can sometimes make children feel cross or grumpy, or all these worries can make children's tummies feel wobbly, or can give them tummy ache. Sometimes all their muddly feelings and thoughts just have to 'leak out'.
>
> If this happens at night when children are asleep, then some children may suddenly need to go to the toilet, or if they are fast asleep they might wet their beds, or they could have muddly, scary dreams and wake up feeling very frightened.
>
> All children can be helped so that their worries don't make them all wobbly inside and they don't 'leak out' in these ways.

> If they just shared their worries with their mum, dad or another grownup they should soon find that their worries are just not so scary after all!
>
> If John has any worries he just needs to share them with his mum and dad. They will understand and together they will be able to help him sort everything out.

- Contact arrangements, whether direct or indirect, should be simply explained making it clear that this was the adults' decision. Children may have some involvement, but it is not their responsibility to write or to respond to letters from birth relatives. The arrangement is between the adults, and if any direct meetings are planned the adoptive parents will be involved.

- Give details of the actual 'Adoption Day' and how this was celebrated, any comments the 'wise judge' made or thoughts he or she may have had! For example, that the judge also realized just how precious and loveable the child was and just how much the adoptive parents loved him or her. Again, scan in photographs.

- Do not end the book here!

3. Present

- Bring the child back to the present, with examples of how well the adopters know and love them and mentions of everyday occurrences, activities and family rituals and routines, which will all help to 'ground' the child.

- Listing and illustrating some of the child's favourite things (e.g. favourite drink, food, colour, book, film, TV programme or toy) will demonstrate just how well the adoptive parents know the child and may prove to be one of the child's favourite pages.

4. Future

- Finally, give the child a positive and compelling future – identify some plans and hopes. This could be planning to join the beavers/brownies or having swimming lessons next month or next year, or the long-term aspiration of becoming a gymnast, an astronaut or a train driver!

- End with a few photographs of life over the last year or so, with the adoptive family, and by thinking about plans for next year, the year after and the year after that and so on, making it clear that the child's future is with the adoptive family.

Chapter 7

Sample Life Story Book: Danny's Life Adventure

Children are unique, as are their stories, so no two books will be the same. It is not a case of 'one size fits all', but the following sample book may inspire further ideas. Note that it is written in the third person using 'child friendly' language, and contains illustrations and positive subliminal messages throughout the 'bite sized' sections.

Danny is fictitious but his story may be familiar, as it is an amalgamation of many children's stories. Danny is five years old and recently adopted, having lived with his adoptive parents for just over a year. His early life was quite chaotic. For much of the time, due to their alcohol and drug abuse, his birth parents were unavailable both emotionally and physically. He has two older sisters who provided some of the 'parenting', but from a very young age Danny learnt not to rely on the adults in his life and he became fairly self-sufficient.

Danny's name was placed on the Child Protection Register shortly after his birth and he was accommodated at the age of two and a half years. He lived in a very busy foster home for over a year, before moving to his adoptive parents. His sisters remain in foster care.

Many of Danny's coping strategies were typical of a child with an avoidant attachment. He found intimacy difficult and was reluctant to accept affection and nurturing. He could be very bossy and his adoptive parents have had to work hard to earn his trust.

Danny's Life Adventure

Contents

2008

1. All about Danny

Danny was born on 1 August 2003, so that makes him five years old at the moment. He is a fine looking boy with a lovely smile, sparkly brown eyes and short dark brown hair.

Danny is a bright, friendly, chatty boy and he is generally very cheerful and happy — and of course his mum and dad think that he is just lovely!

Danny is just about the right height and the right build for a five year old. He is fit and healthy, with plenty of energy, so he is usually very busy. He loves cycling or scooting to the park, at the end of his road, with his mum and dad. Sometimes he meets his friends there and they play football, have running races or climb trees — and Danny loves to organize everyone! On sunny days they have a picnic or a barbeque and then Danny knows this is something that the grownups are in charge of!

Danny prefers to be outside but when indoors he likes to play with his dinosaur collection or his toy cars, and he also likes drawing and painting. Sometimes he plays on the computer or watches television, but Danny doesn't like to sit still for too long. Of course, some quiet times are very good for any growing boy, so his mum is helping him with this, and now Danny really enjoys snuggling up on the settee, just the two of them, and having special story times.

2. Danny's Home and Family

Danny lives with his mum, his dad and his sister Jane, in Newtown. They all live in a three-bedroomed house. Danny has his own bedroom — it's the one at the front in the photograph. He has dinosaur wallpaper, a dinosaur duvet cover, a dinosaur rug, a dinosaur lamp — and I think I can even see one of his dinosaurs peeping out of that window!

This is Danny with his mum and dad. His mum's name is Sandra and his dad is called Tom.

Danny's sister is Jane. Jane is four years older than Danny, so she is nine years old at the moment. Most of the time Danny and Jane play well together, but Mum says that sometimes they can have their 'off days' too. I wonder what she means?

Danny also has grandparents. There is Nana and Pops. That Mum's mum and dad. And there is Granny and Grandpa, and that's Dad's mum and dad. They live quite a long way away but sometimes they come to Danny's house for Sunday lunch or Danny goes to see them.

And finally we mustn't forget the other member of the family – Tiger – the cat.

This is Danny with all of his family on holiday last year. They were on the beach in Devon.

This was Danny's first seaside holiday. He loved building sandcastles but the sea was just too cold! Danny thinks that swimming in a pool is much warmer, and his sister Jane agrees!

3. St Paul's School

Danny goes to St Paul's Infants School and his sister goes to the school next door – St Paul's Junior School. The schools are quite close to Danny's home, so he

and Jane can scoot there and back every day. His mum always makes sure that they arrive in plenty of time in the morning. Every afternoon, when school finishes, Mum or Dad is waiting for him by the school gate, and then together they go to collect Jane from her school.

Last term Danny's teacher was Mrs Baker. She was a very nice lady, with lots of patience, so she didn't usually get cross with any of the children. Danny likes

Mrs Baker because she smiles at him every morning and says, 'Hello Danny. How are you?' His teacher really likes Danny too, and told his mum that he is a lovely boy to have in the classroom and she is really going to miss him next term when he moves to Mrs Jones' class. Luckily, Danny has heard that Mrs Jones is a very nice teacher too!

Danny is good at numbers and he likes art and computer work best. Some of his reading books and the spellings he had to learn last year were very hard, but he had a good school report and the teacher said that he always tries his best and works hard. Mrs Baker also said that Danny is now much better at asking the teacher for help when he

doesn't quite understand what he has to do. He has a certificate for this. So well done Danny!

Perhaps the best part of school is play time and then Danny can play football. Danny has lots of school friends. There is Fred, Toby, Owen, Wing, Jo, Grant, Kath and Sian — and there are a few others too. What a lot of different names!

4. Danny's Name

Danny's name is actually Daniel but he is usually called Danny — and he likes this. His full name is Daniel Anthony Davies and this is a copy of his birth certificate.

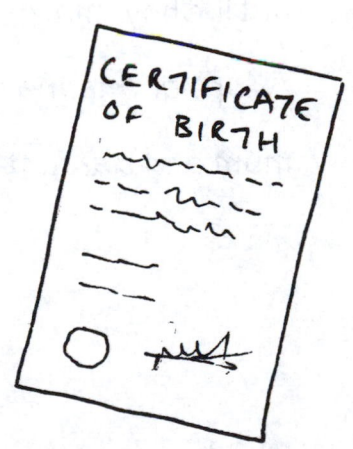

Of course, Danny's name was not always Daniel Anthony Davies. At first, it was Daniel Smith. How can this be? Well, families come in all shapes and sizes and children join families in all sorts of ways. Some are born into them, some live with step parents or with aunts and uncles, grandparents or friends, or with special guardians. Some children live with foster carers, while some are adopted into their families.

Foster carers sometimes look after older children for a long time, but they usually only look after young children for a short while, either until they go home or until they move to a new family to be adopted. Adoption means that children stay with their new mum and dad until they are all grown up.

Many famous people and characters have been adopted, like Moses in the Bible, Superman, Stuart Little the mouse, Paddington Bear and Babe the pig. Danny's sister, Jane, is also adopted, his cousin Clive is adopted and there are many other adopted children living in Newtown and indeed all over the world! So, like thousands of other children, Danny was adopted and this is how Danny became:

Daniel Anthony Davies

5. The Beginning

Danny was born on 1 August 2003, and like most babies he was born in hospital. He was born in West Hospital in London at 7.30 in the morning, so just in time for breakfast, and as it was summertime it was a nice warm day.

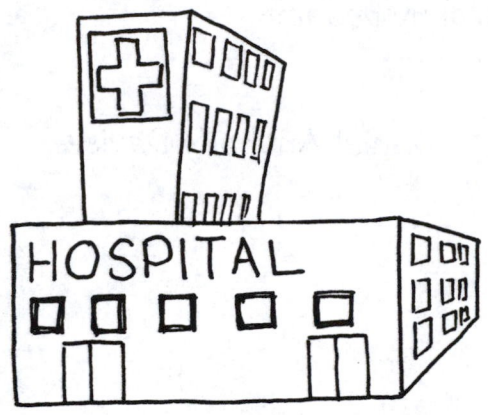

Danny weighed 2.5 kgs, and that is 5.5 pounds or the same as two and a half bags of sugar. This is quite small for a newborn baby and so, for the first two weeks, Danny was in a special cot — an incubator — as he needed extra care.

The first of August was a Friday, so according to the children's rhyme Danny is 'loving and giving'. The August flower is a gladiolus and the birth stone is peridot. This is a precious green gem.

Danny's birth sign is Leo, the lion. People with this birth sign are said to be generous, warm-hearted, kind and enthusiastic, but sometimes they can be a bit bossy too! I wonder if this sounds a bit like Danny?

Like all newborn babies Danny had a birth mother and a birth father. Danny's birth mother is called Ann Burton and his birth father is David Smith. When Danny was born, Ann and David were very happy and they both thought that he was a lovely and very loveable baby, and they phoned their family and friends to let them know that their gorgeous baby boy had arrived.

They decided to name their baby Daniel Smith. Ann chose the name Daniel as that was her grandfather's name, and Smith as this was David's surname.

Ann has brown eyes and when Danny was born she had long dark hair, but she later had it cut short and sometimes she changed the colour too. Ann was born in South London in 1974, so she was 29 years old when Danny was born. She wasn't very tall – just over 5 ft – and slim, and sometimes she wore glasses. She liked school and had done well passing lots of exams. When she left she worked in an office for a while and then in a shop. Ann was a friendly lady and she enjoyed going out and dancing.

David was much taller than Ann – he was nearly 6 ft – and he was well built. He had light brown hair and blue eyes. David was born a year before Ann in 1973, so he was 30 years old when Danny

was born. David was born in Liverpool but moved to London with his family when he was very young. David didn't enjoy school very much and when he left he started to train as a gardener as he liked being outside, but then he changed his mind and worked in a garage. When he was 19 years old, he started to work at a supermarket and this is where he met Ann.

6. Staying with Alice and Ken

Ann and David decided to live together soon after they met and at first they were very happy. They were delighted when their first child, Laura, was born in 1993 and when their second daughter, Jade, was born a year later, but gradually things started to go wrong. Ann and David were arguing too much and this must have been very scary for the girls. Sometimes David would get so cross he would lose his temper and then he would hurt Ann. Sometimes the neighbours heard the shouting and they would telephone the police. Then the police and the social workers would come to the house to calm everyone down, and to make sure that Laura and Jade were okay.

Perhaps it was because Ann and David were feeling unhappy that they began drinking cans of lager, as they thought that this would help. When this didn't make them feel any better they began taking drugs. Again they thought that taking drugs would make them happier, but of course all it did was make everything much, much worse! In fact, sometimes the lager and the drugs made them feel very ill and very sleepy – and even more unhappy!

When Ann knew that she was going to have another baby she was very pleased, but sadly she was still taking some drugs, and this is why Danny needed

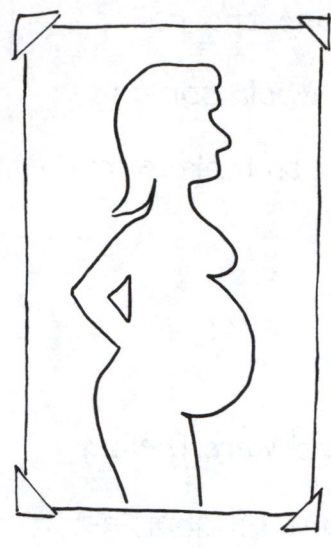

special care when he was first born. The drugs that had sometimes made Ann feel unwell had also made little baby Danny feel ill while he was growing inside Ann. They also made him unwell when he was first born and he needed special medicine to help him feel better.

Thankfully Danny was soon well enough to leave hospital and the whole family were really pleased when he went home. Laura was ten years old and Jade was nine years old at that time, and although they were in school for some of the time, when they were home they liked helping Ann to look after baby Danny. Although they were only young children too, sometimes, especially when Ann and David were feeling ill, they would bath and feed the baby and put him to bed.

Danny had his first birthday and then his second birthday with Ann, David and his sisters, but by this time many people – the doctors, the health visitors, the teachers at Laura and Jade's school, the police and the social workers – were becoming very worried about all the children, but especially little Danny. Ann and David were just not looking after him properly and not giving him all the time and attention that babies must have, so baby Danny just wasn't growing as much as he should.

In fact, Ann and David were not looking after any of the children very well. The home was dirty and messy, there were no clean clothes, the girls were missing lots of school because Ann and David didn't make sure that they were up in time in the mornings, and sometimes there was no food in the house so they were often very hungry. Perhaps instead of buying food Ann and David were using their money to buy drugs – and they cost a lot of money! So the grownups were just not looking after the children properly. This must have been very frightening and scary for all of them.

One day the social worker and the police called at the house and found the children on their own. The children were hungry, cold and dirty. Everyone agreed that it was just too dangerous for them to live with Ann and David any longer. Little Danny looked very ill and he had a big bruise on his head so he was taken to hospital, while Jade and Laura went to stay with a foster carer, Pam. Pam would look after them properly and make sure that they were safe.

At the hospital the doctors looked at Danny's head. Ann and David came to the hospital to see Danny too, but they didn't know how he had hurt himself. The police and social workers spoke to Ann and David and told them that they should never leave children in the house on their own, as this is very dangerous. Children need grownups to look after them all the time.

Danny stayed in hospital overnight to make sure that he was okay, and then he went to stay with foster carers too. He went to stay with Alice and Ken.

Alice and Ken had looked after lots of babies and little children and they took very good care of Danny. It must have been quite scary at first and I expect that he missed everyone. He was very pleased when Jade and Laura came to visit him with their foster carer and every week the social worker, Jaz, would come in her car and take him to the play room at the Children's Centre to see Ann and David.

At the foster home Danny grew really quickly. He put on weight and became much taller, and he really liked playing with Sam and Sally. Sam and Sally were twins, and they had been living with Alice and Ken for quite a long time. Danny was sad when the time came for them to leave, but Alice and Ken told him not to worry because the twins were very pleased to be moving to a new family all of their own – an adoptive family.

7. Building Strong Walls

Bringing up children is a bit like building a wall. To make tall, strong walls you need a very good

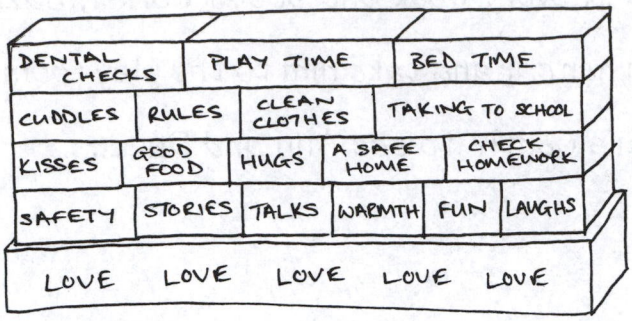

foundation and then, using just the right type and just the right amount of cement, you carefully lay all the different bricks on top. The cement is like the love that holds everything else together and makes the wall strong. You can see from this wall of bricks that children need love, but they also need lots of different kinds of caring to help them grow properly, and they need to be cared for by grownups who can make sure that children are happy, healthy and safe.

Ann and David loved all of their children, but they were not able to look after themselves properly or do all the other things that parents must do to keep their children safe and to help them grow into strong, healthy grownups.

While the children were being cared for at their foster homes, the social workers and the doctors tried to help Ann and David. If they could stop taking drugs they might be able to look after their children again, but sadly this was too hard for them and although they tried, neither of them seemed able to do this.

The social workers had lots of meetings and long talks about Danny, Laura and Jade. No one thought that they should go back to Ann and David, so they went to the court to see the judge. Judges are very

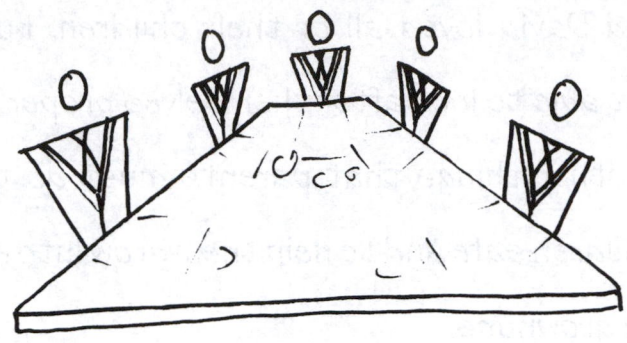

clever and very wise. The judge listened to everyone — to all the workers and to David and Ann. The judge agreed that the children should not live with their birth parents because they just didn't know how to look after them. The judge also thought that as Laura and Jade were older they should stay with their foster carer, Pam.

As Danny was so young, the judge felt that he needed a new family — one with a mum and dad who would be able to understand Danny and would know just how to look after him and keep him safe for a very, very long time – until he was all grown up!

Everyone thought that when Danny moved to his new family, he should still see Laura and Jade sometimes, but he wouldn't go to the Children's Centre to see Ann and David any more. Ann and David still cared about Danny and they wanted to know that he was well and happy, so it was also agreed that his new mum and dad could write to Ann and David and sometimes send some photographs to them, so that they would know that Danny was okay and growing into a fine boy. In turn, Ann and David could write to Danny's mum and dad to share their news.

8. The Davies Family

Sandra and Tom were just the right grownups to be Danny's mum and dad. They knew what to do to help him to grow into a healthy, strong child – just like that strong brick wall. They knew that children need lots of love and cuddles, plenty of sleep and good food, a warm house, clean clothes, lots of fun, games and play times, and just the right number of rules to make sure that they are safe and secure.

Sandra and Tom fell in love with Danny as soon as they saw him. You could say that it was 'love at first sight'. They were so happy, although Danny was a little worried and looked very unsure at first. They gave him a very soft, furry toy puppy dog. Danny was only little and he couldn't say puppy at that time, so he called it 'putty' instead. Putty has had lots of cuddles from Danny since then and although he is not quite so furry now he still sits at the end of Danny's bed every night.

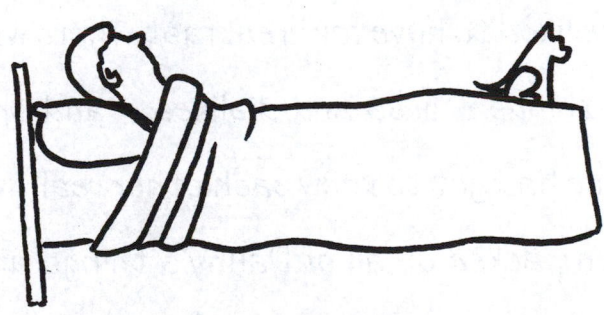

Sandra and Tom visited Danny every day after this and sometimes Jane came too. On one of the days Jade and Laura arrived with their foster carer, Pam. They all exchanged presents and had a special tea party. Danny's mum and dad were pleased to meet them and Jade and Laura were very pleased to meet Danny's new mum and dad too and they took lots of photographs.

Alice told Danny's mum and dad all about him and about the things he liked doing and eating, and what time he went to bed and what time he got up, and what he liked to have for breakfast. There was a huge list of things – likes and dislikes – and then, when everyone had got to know each other really well, Alice and Ken packed up all of Danny's things and helped his mum and dad to put them all into their car. It was quite a squash! Then Mum, Dad, Jane and Danny drove all the way from London to Newtown — and that's quite a long way, over 100 miles.

So Danny joined the Davies family at the beginning of 2007, when he was three and a half years old, and that was how Danny became Sandra and Tom's son, and how they became his mum and dad.

Of course it was very strange for Danny when he first moved to his new home. Danny had to get used to the new house: the rooms looked different, the furniture was different, the smells were different, his clothes felt different, the food was different, there were different Davies ways of doing things, they even had different words for some things, and he had a new sister, Jane! What a lot of different things for a little boy to get used to!

At first it must have been very strange, confusing and perhaps a bit worrying for Danny. His mum and dad could understand all this and they knew that, in time, with their love and care they would help Danny to feel safe, settled and loved.

Of course it must have been a bit worrying for Jane too. She had been adopted into the Davies family when she was two years old. Some children worry about having a new brother or sister and think that perhaps their mum and dad will not love them as much. I wonder if Jane worried about this too? Of course she needn't have worried! Jane and Danny's mum and dad have very big hearts and their love just keeps on growing and growing and growing so there will always be plenty of love for both of them.

9. The Wise Judge

After Danny had lived with his mum and dad for quite a long time, and when everyone knew each other very well, they all went to the court to see that very wise judge. All of the Davies family went. Mum, Dad, Jane, and the social worker, Liz, and of course the most important person that day – Danny. It was a very special occasion and everyone had the day off work and school to be there.

They all went to see the wise judge in the Newtown Court in July 2008, a few weeks before Danny's fifth birthday.

The judge had already read all about Danny, and he knew just how loveable and precious he was and he said that Danny deserved loving, caring parents and he could see that Sandra and Tom loved him very much. So the judge said that Danny should definitely be adopted, and remain part of the Davies family forever.

Mum and Dad liked the name Anthony so they told the judge that they would like this to be Danny's new middle name. The judge liked the name too and he agreed and he signed the 'Adoption Order' and Danny officially and legally became

Daniel Anthony Davies

To celebrate the Adoption Day they caught the train to London and they went on the London Eye. Afterwards they had a special meal with Granny and Grandpa, and Nana and Pops.

10. More about Danny

Danny has been living with his mum and dad for quite a long time now and every day he is growing taller and stronger. He is a very important member of the Davies family and although he can still be a bit bossy at times he is beginning to realize that his mum and dad are very good at organizing everything and doing all the things that grownups should do to keep him safe. Most importantly, Danny's mum and dad know him so well, they understand him, they look after him, they know just what he needs, and they love him dearly...

In fact Danny's mum and dad know all sorts of very important things about Danny. For instance, they know that Danny's...

favourite football club is Arsenal

favourite TV programme is Scooby-Doo

favourite book is Horrid Henry

favourite food is Mum's sponge cake and her roast chicken dinners favourite drink is banana milkshake

favourite colour is red

favourite bedtime is being tucked in very tightly by Mum and having a bedtime story.

So, you can see Danny's mum and dad certainly know lots and lots about Danny!

Danny is still a very busy boy with plenty of energy and he has lots of plans for the future too. He is having another holiday this summer. The Davies family will be going to the seaside in Devon again. I wonder if the sea will be any warmer this year? Mum says that perhaps next year they might go to Spain for their holiday as the sea is very blue and very warm there, so Danny likes the sound of that!

Danny, Mum, Dad and Jane will be going to see Jade, Laura and Pam again soon. They are all going bowling and for a meal afterwards! Danny hopes it will be a hamburger! I wonder? And then, when Danny goes back to school he will have swimming lessons and he is also going to join the cubs with his friends, Toby and Owen, so that will be more fun!

When he is grown up, Danny thinks he would like to be a footballer or a dog walker or he might like to fly an aeroplane! He is not quite sure yet, so he could change his mind about this. I wonder?

But there are some things that I certainly don't need to wonder about!

I just know for sure that whatever Danny does in the future his mum and dad will always be there to help him, to guide him and to love him. They will always be his mum and dad, and Danny will always be their very, very precious son...

forever and ever and ever...

And I just know for sure that although this may seem like the end of Danny's book, Danny's great life adventure will...

go on and on and on...

Chapter 8

Final Thoughts

There is clearly a moral and a legal duty to gather photographs and record as much information as possible about members of the birth family and other significant adults in the child's history. The Adoption and Children Act 2002 highlighted the need for adopted children to be given comprehensive information about themselves, and Schedule 5 of the Adoption Agency Regulations 2005 refers specifically to the provision of later life letters and life story books. A clear account of the family history and the circumstances leading to the child being accommodated and adopted is both vital for the child and a legal requirement.

Whilst this new format for the child's life story book – present → past→ present→ future – is not suitable for all accommodated children, for those for whom permanency, and adoption in particular, is the plan, this is likely to be the most appropriate model. This means that the book will not be finalized until some time after the permanent placement or after the adoption hearing.

This approach will call for 'inter-team' and, in some instances, inter-agency co-operation and commitment. Someone will need to take responsibility for co-ordinating and finishing the book. This responsibility is likely to lie with the family placement/adoption workers, as in many agencies they will continue to have some contact with the adoptive family for a period of at least a year following the adoption hearing. But the very important 'middle' section, with information about the birth, the birth parents, the circumstances leading to the child being accommodated and previous fostering placements, will need to be available pre-adoption placement.

The social workers will each have a different, but equally valuable, perspective on the child's life. They each hold some knowledge of the child's history and present circumstances. These different elements must be presented in a coherent way, so that the child's sense of self becomes more positive and integrated, and their understanding of their own history becomes less fragmented.

The book is about the child's life and it is written for the child, so it should provide a simple, honest, coherent narrative. It is just the first 'tier' and, although this alone will not ensure that a child has a clear understanding of their history, it is a good starting point. The book is just a basic tool for adopters to build on, at the child's pace.

There are lessons to be learnt from our knowledge and work with adopted adults and the 'closed' adoptions of the past. Their 'need to know' and to find the 'missing pieces of the jigsaw' are well documented, but there is also a danger of overcompensating for these past secretive adoptions and overwhelming today's adoptees with too much detail.

The life story book needs to be child friendly and, whilst acknowledging the difficulties, sadness and losses experienced, it should also be a celebration of the child's life. The book should leave the child with a positive sense of who they are and with hope for the future – not weighed down and overburdened by the birth parents' troubled history.

If time and effort is put into creating a sensitive life story book that can be used with confidence by the adoptive parents, then the book will achieve its purpose – and the social workers involved will have made an important contribution to helping the child move towards the positive future that he or she certainly deserves.

References

Bowlby, J. (1992) *A Secure Base: Clinical Applications of Attachment Theory.* London: Routledge.

Bowlby, J. (2007) *The Making and Breaking of Affectional Bonds.* London: Routledge.

Burnell, A. and Vaughan, J. (2008) 'Remembering never to forget and forgetting never to remember: Re-thinking life story work.' In B. Luckock and M. Lefevre (2008) *Direct Work: Social Work with Children and Young People in Care.* London: British Agencies for Adoption and Fostering.

Fahlberg, V. (2003) *A Child's Journey through Placement.* London: British Agencies for Adoption and Fostering.

O'Malley, B. (2004) *Lifebooks: Creating A Treasure for The Adopted Child.* Winthrop, MA: Adoptions-Works.

Rose, R. and Philpot, T. (2005) *The Child's Own Story: Life Story Work with Traumatized Children.* London: Jessica Kingsley Publishers.

Ryan, T. and Walker, R. (2007) *Life Story Work.* London: British Agencies for Adoption and Fostering.

van Gulden, H. and Riedel, C. (1998–1999) *In Search of Self: Reclaiming and Healing the Lost, Wounded and Missing Parts of Self.* Minneapolis, MN: Adoptive Family Counseling Center.

Further Reading

Archer, C. (1999) *First Steps in Parenting the Child Who Hurts: Tiddlers and Toddlers.* London: Jessica Kingsley Publishers.

Archer, C. (1999) *Next Steps in Parenting the Child Who Hurts: Tykes and Teens.* London: Jessica Kingsley Publishers.

Archer, C. and Burnell, A. (2003) *Trauma Attachment and Family Permanence.* London: Jessica Kingsley Publishers.

Archer, C. and Gordon, C. (2006) *New Families, Old Scripts: A Guide to the Language of Trauma and Attachment in Adoptive Families.* London: Jessica Kingsley Publishers.

Bowlby, J. (1992) *A Secure Base: Clinical Applications of Attachment Theory.* London: Routledge.

Bowlby, J. (2007) *The Making and Breaking of Affectional Bonds.* London: Routledge.

Fahlberg, V. (2003) *A Child's Journey through Placement.* London: British Agencies for Adoption and Fostering.

Foster, C. (2008) *Big Steps for Little People: Parenting Your Adopted Child.* London: Jessica Kingsley Publishers.

Grinder, M. (2007) *The Elusive Obvious: The Science of Non- verbal Communication.* Battle Ground, WA: Michael Grinder & Associates.

Hughes, D. (2004) *Building the Bonds of Attachment: Awakening Love in Deeply Troubled Children.* Lanham, MD: Rowman & Littlefield.

Hughes, D. (2007) *Attachment-Focused Family Therapy.* New York: W.W. Norton & Company.

Lacher, D., Nichols, T. and May, J. (2005) *Connecting with Kids through Stories: Using Narratives to Facilitate Attachment in Adopted Children.* London: Jessica Kingsley Publishers.

Luckock, B. and Lefevre, M. (2008) *Direct Work: Social Work with Children and Young People in Care.* London: British Agencies for Adoption and Fostering.

MacLeod, J. and Macrae, S. (2006) *Adoption Parenting: Creating a Toolbox, Building Connections.* Warren, NJ: EMK Press.

O'Malley, B. (2004) *Lifebooks: Creating A Treasure for The Adopted Child.* Winthrop, MA: Adoptions-Works.

Romaine, M., Turley, T. and Tuckey, N. (2007) *Preparing Children for Permanence.* London: British Agencies for Adoption and Fostering.

Rose, R. and Philpot, T. (2005) *The Child's Own Story: Life Story Work with Traumatized Children.* London: Jessica Kingsley Publishers.

Rosen, S, (1991) *My Voice Will Go With You: The Teaching Tales of Milton H. Erickson.* London: Norton.

Ryan, T. and Walker, R. (2007) *Life Story Work.* London: British Agencies for Adoption and Fostering.

van Gulden, H. and Reidel, C. (1998–1999) *In Search of Self: Reclaiming and Healing the Lost, Wounded and Missing Parts of Self.* Minneapolis: MN: Adoptive Family Counseling Center.

Index